This book belongs to:

____

Elephant

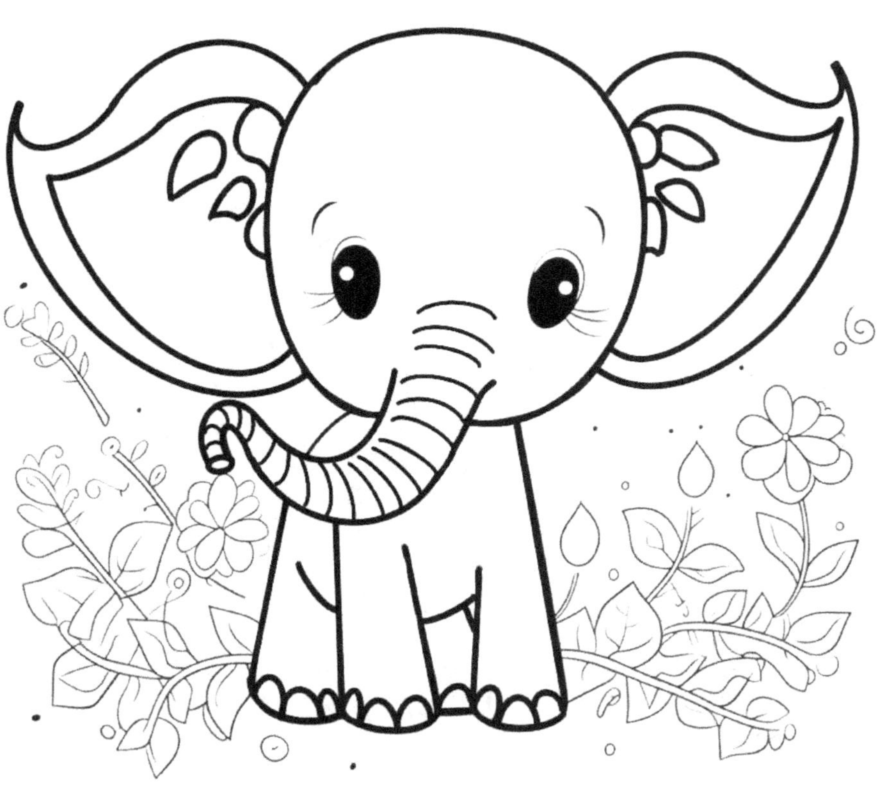

Lion

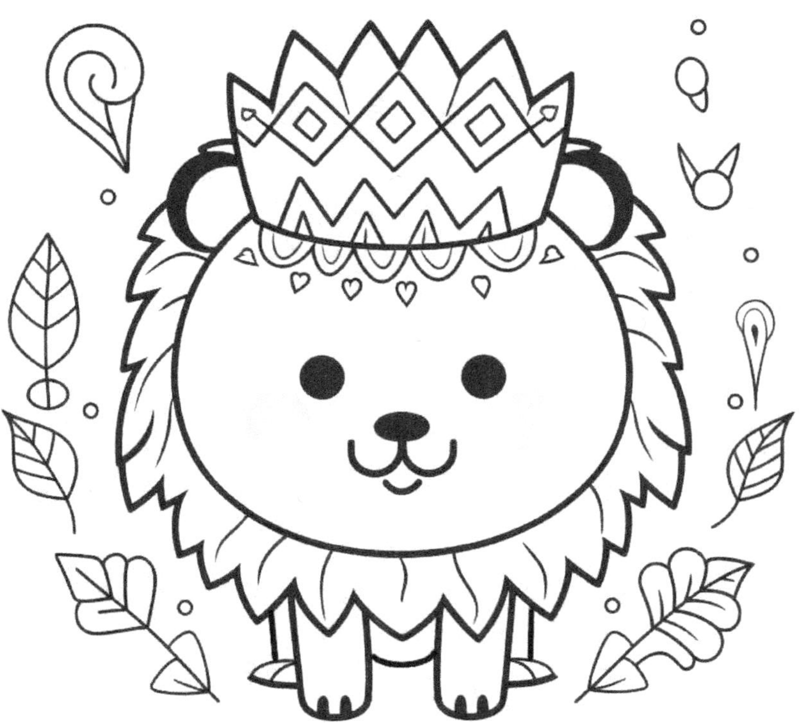

Cow

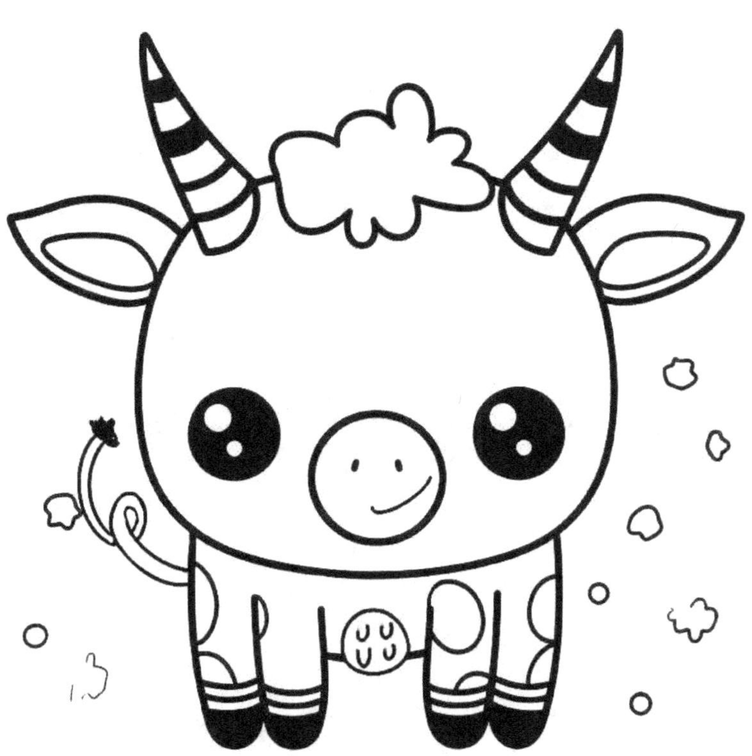

Ostrich

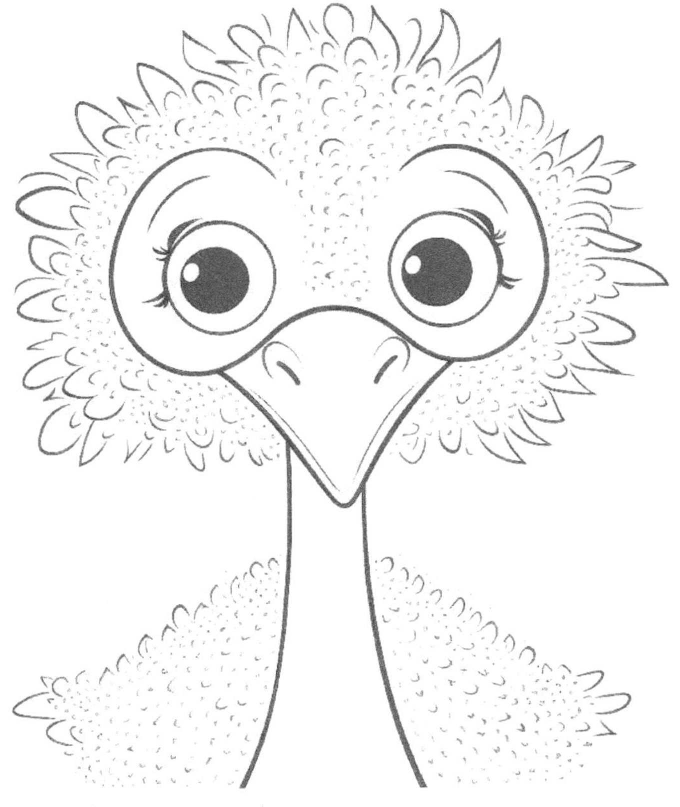

Dog

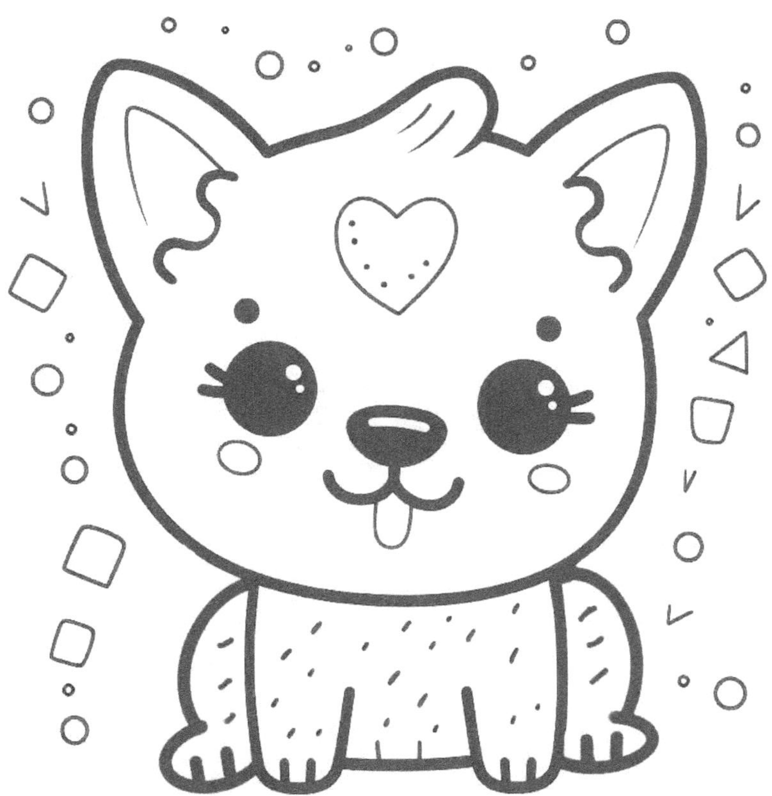

Duck

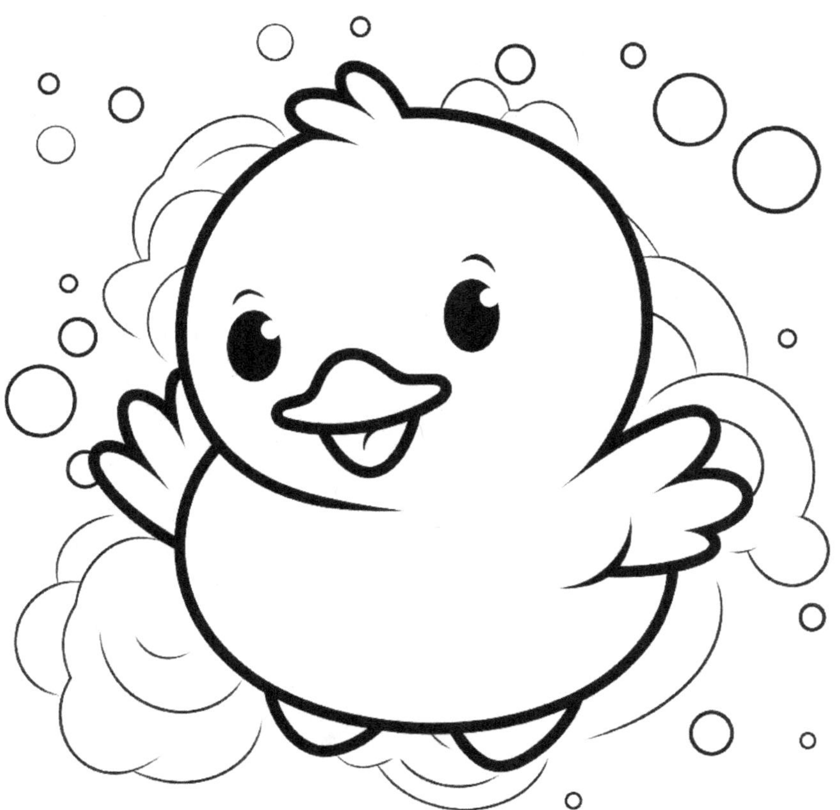

Cat

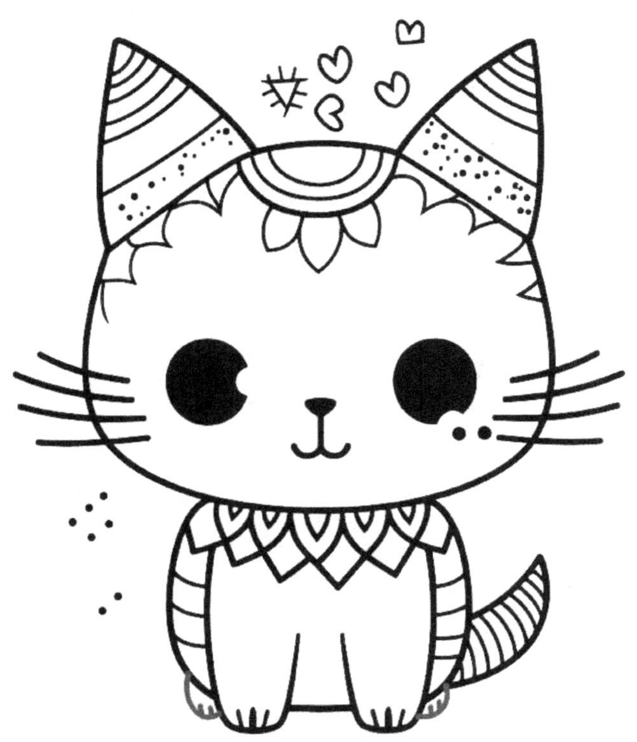

Bunny

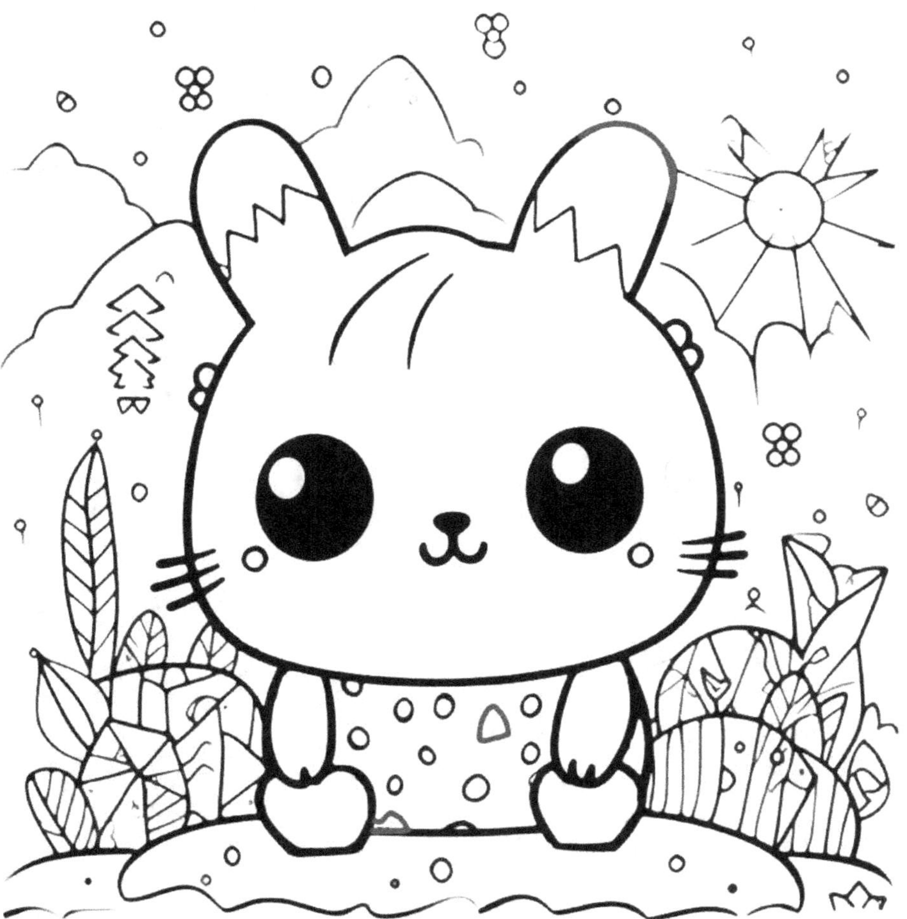

Bear

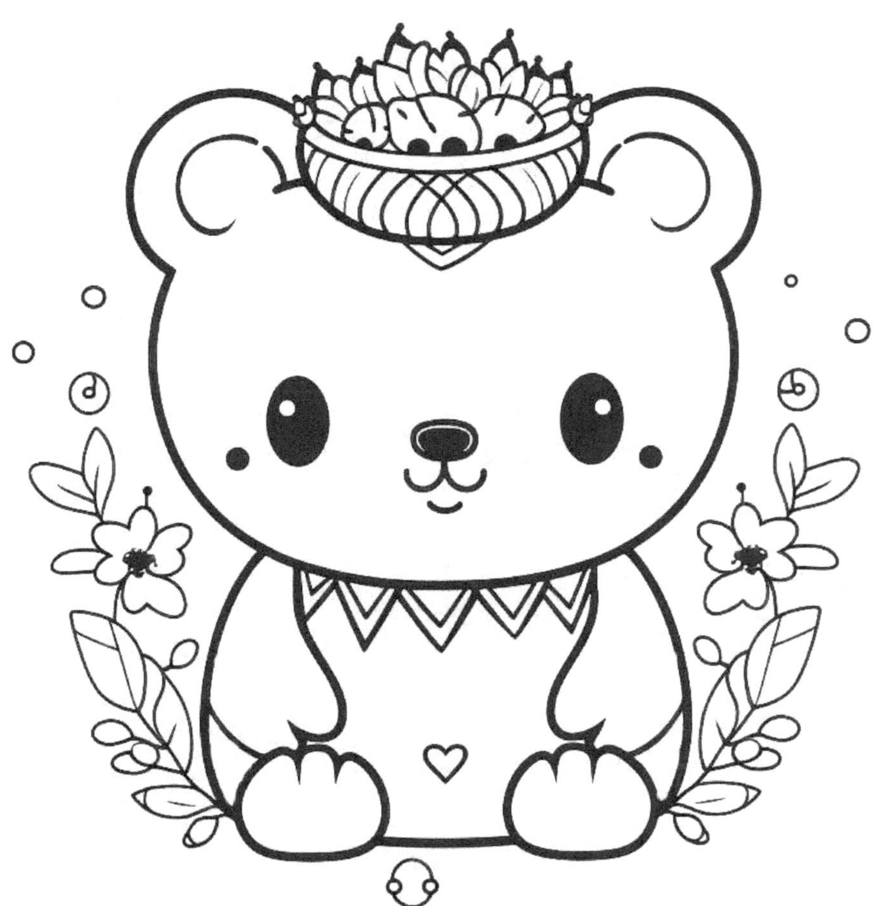

Giraffe

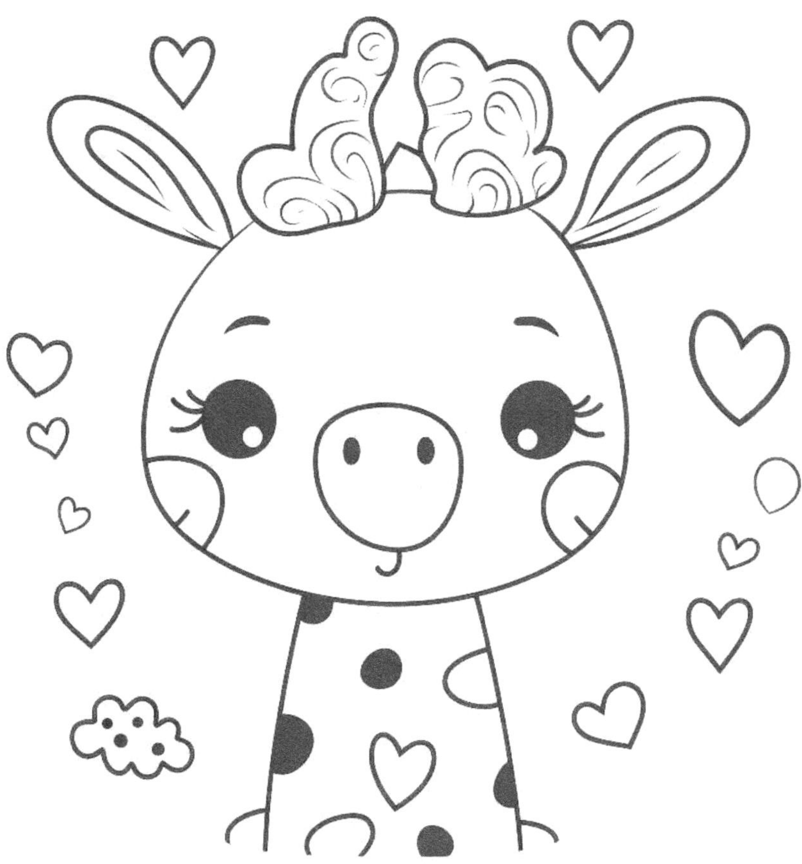

Tiger

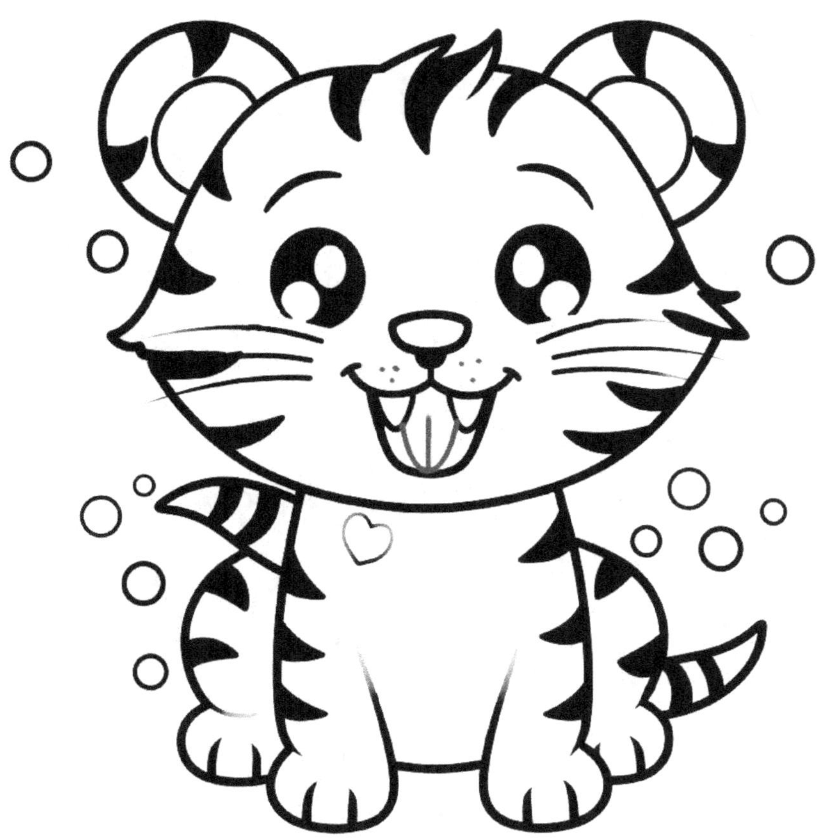

Sheep

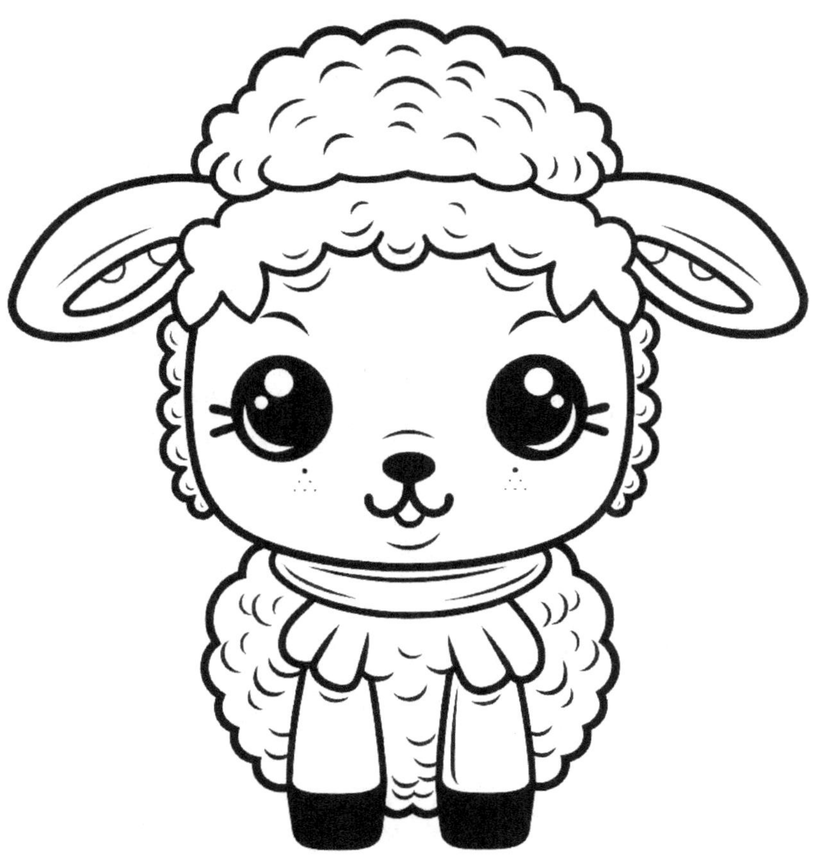

Bat

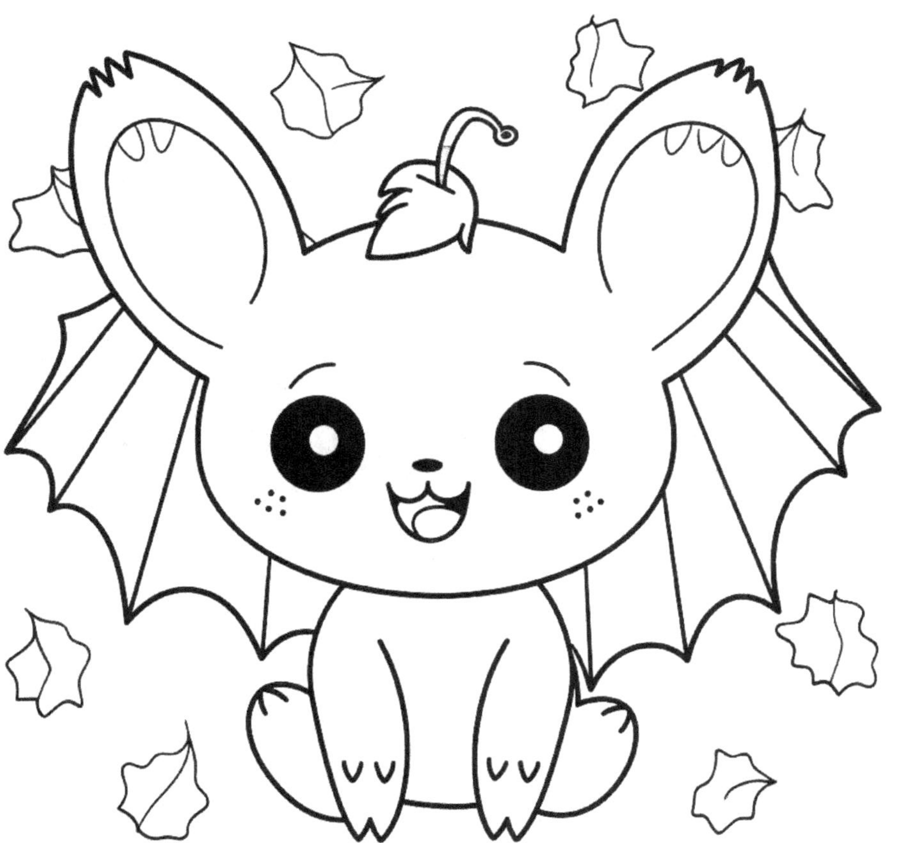

Monkey

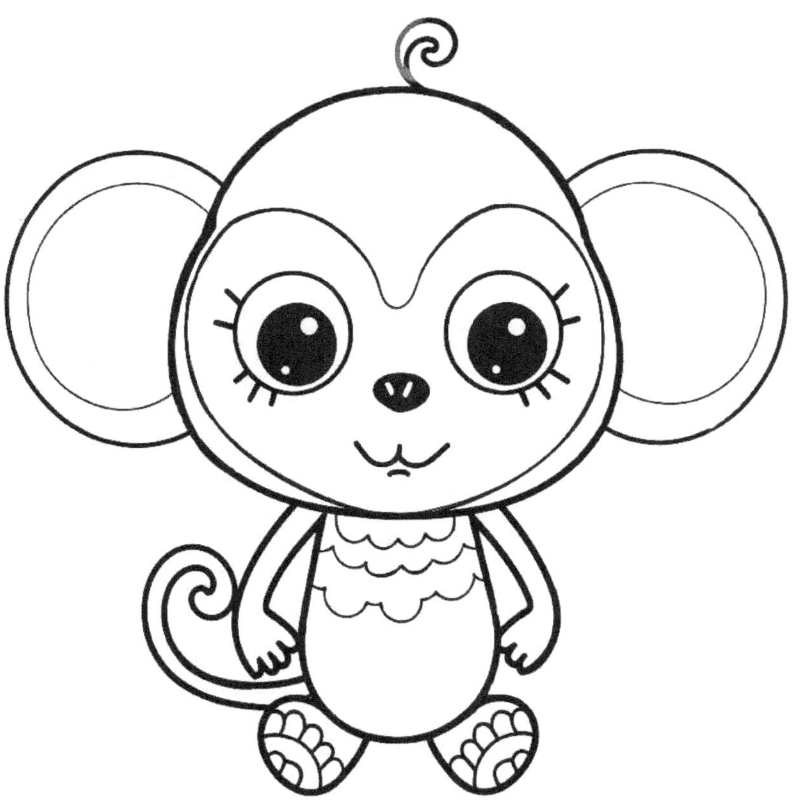

Bird

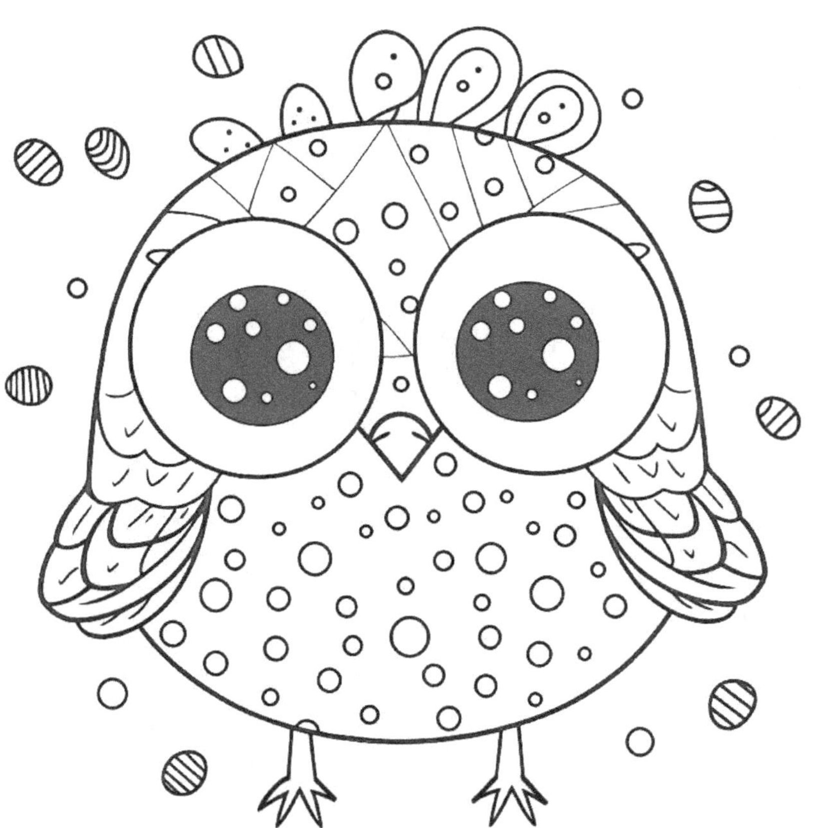

Fish

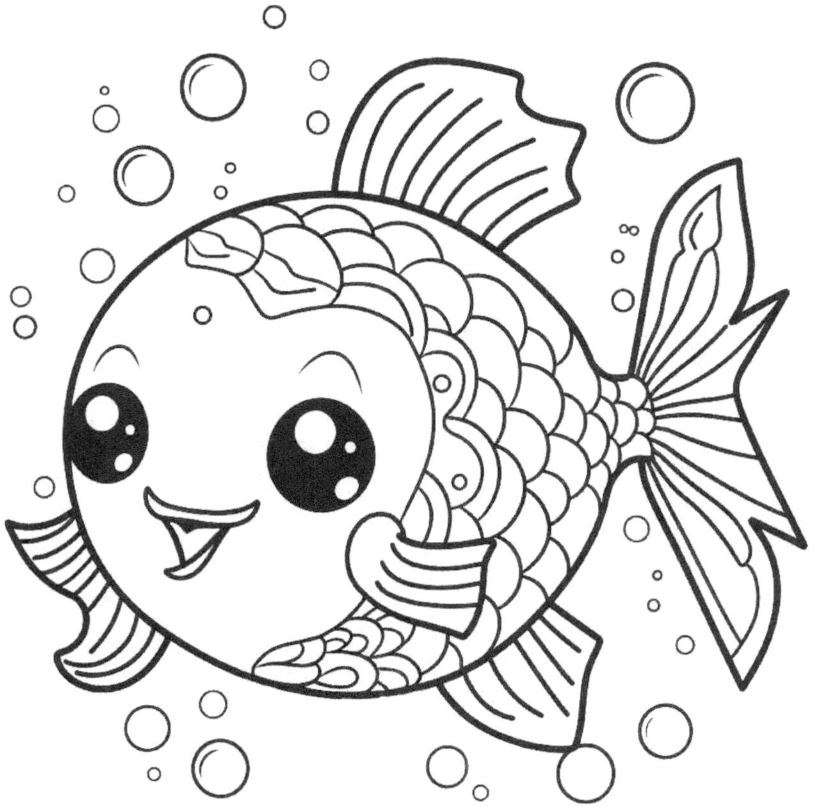

Crocodile

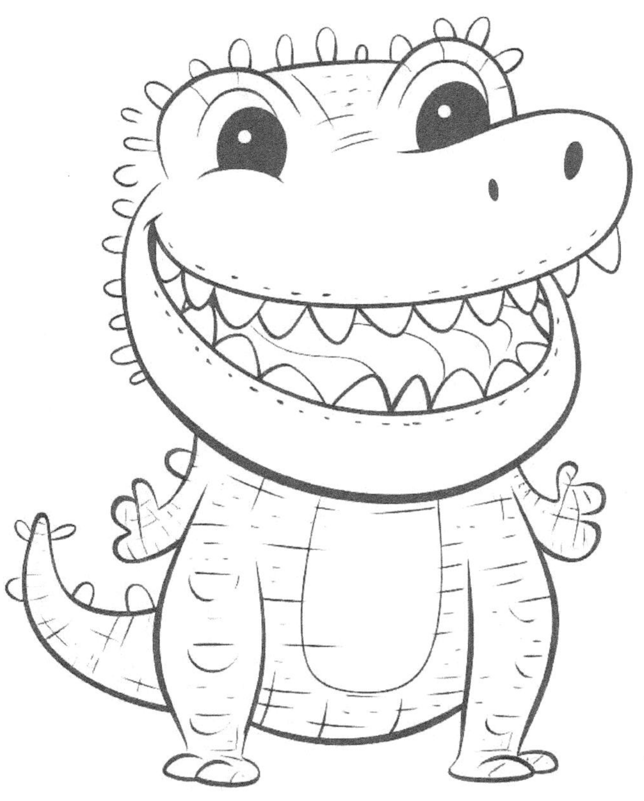

Bee

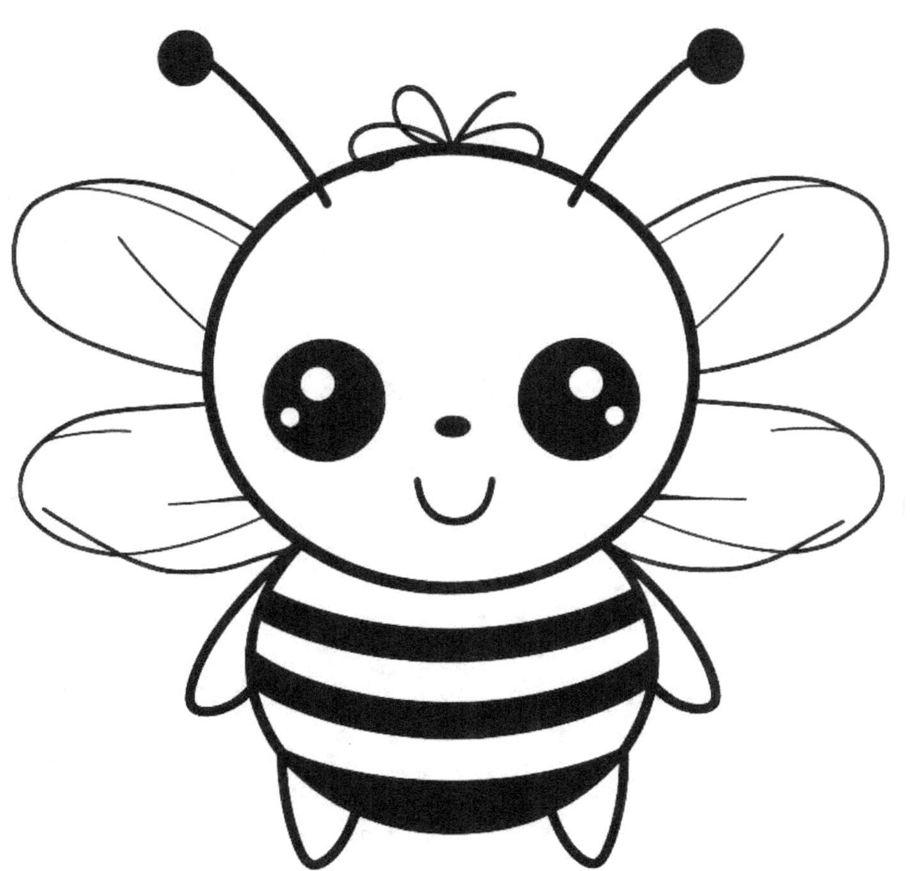

Octopus

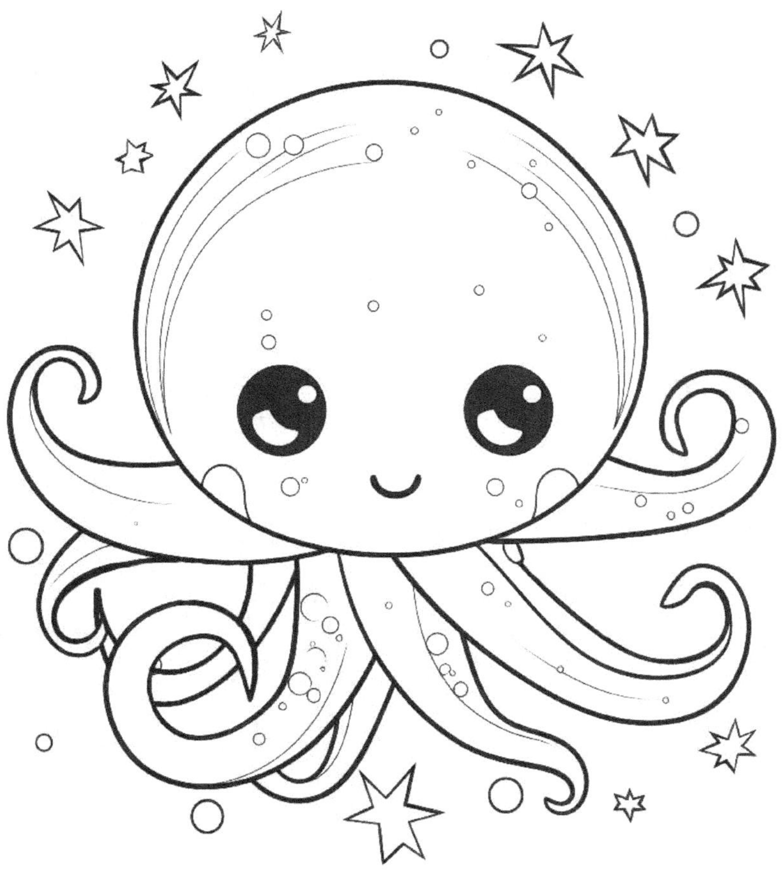

Hippopotamus

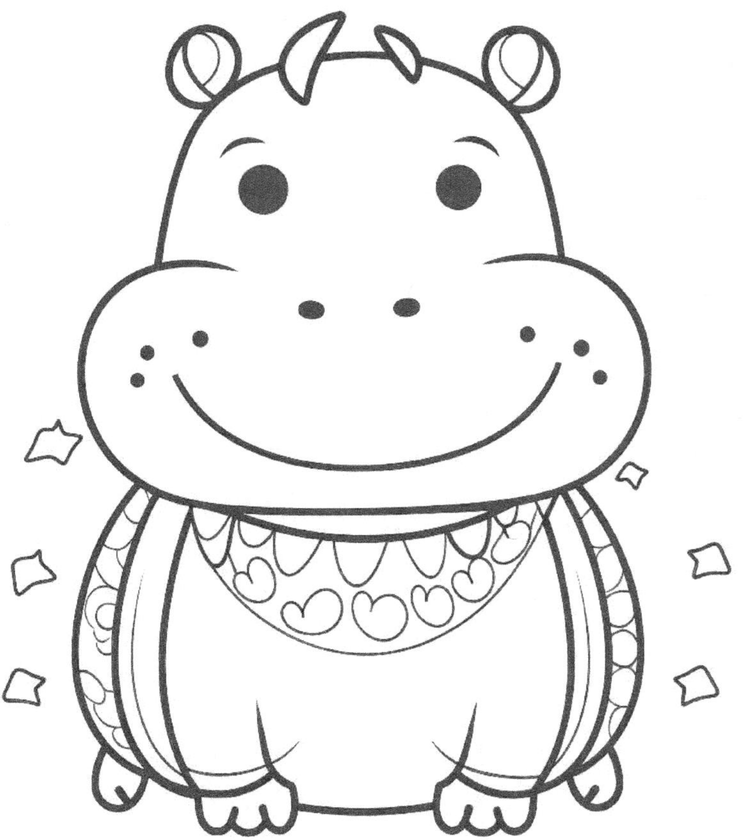

Koala

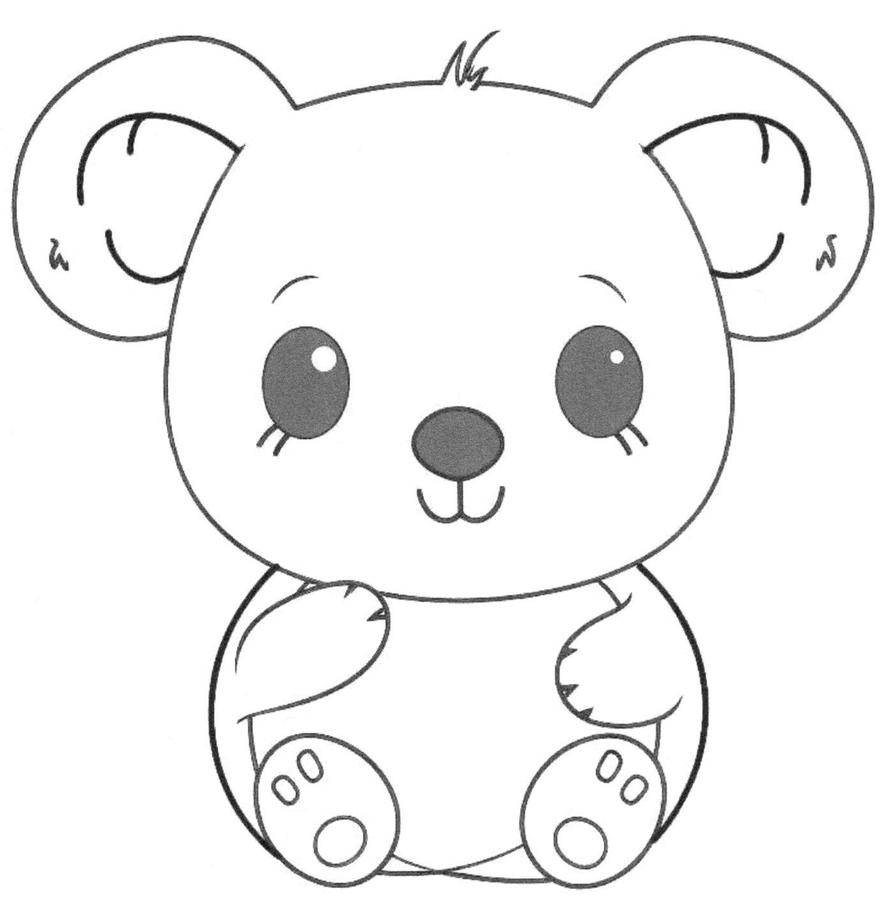

Kangaroo

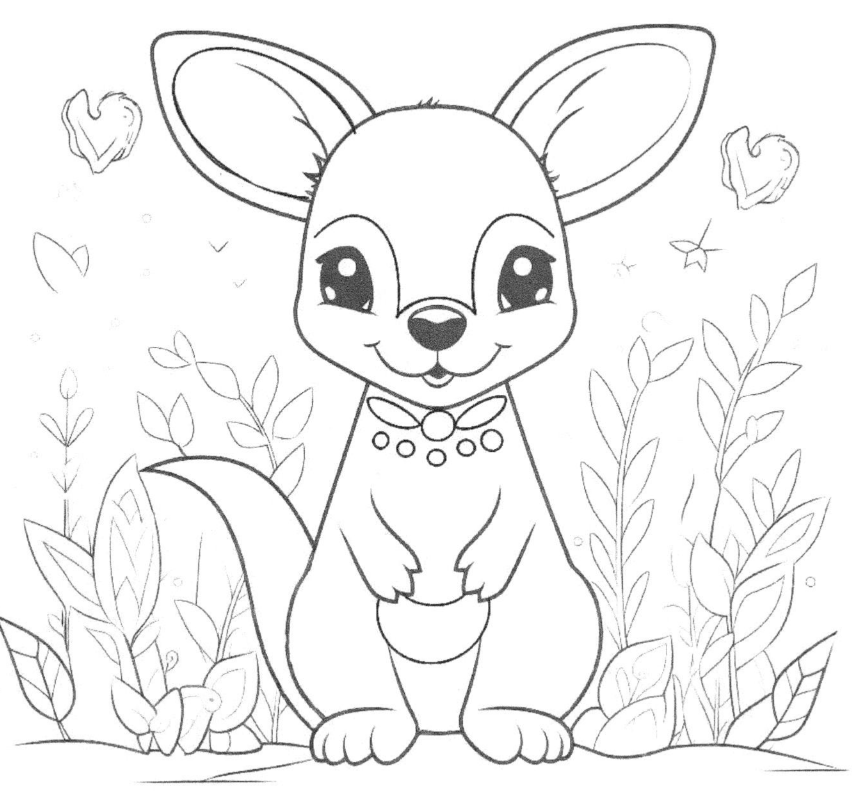

Lizard

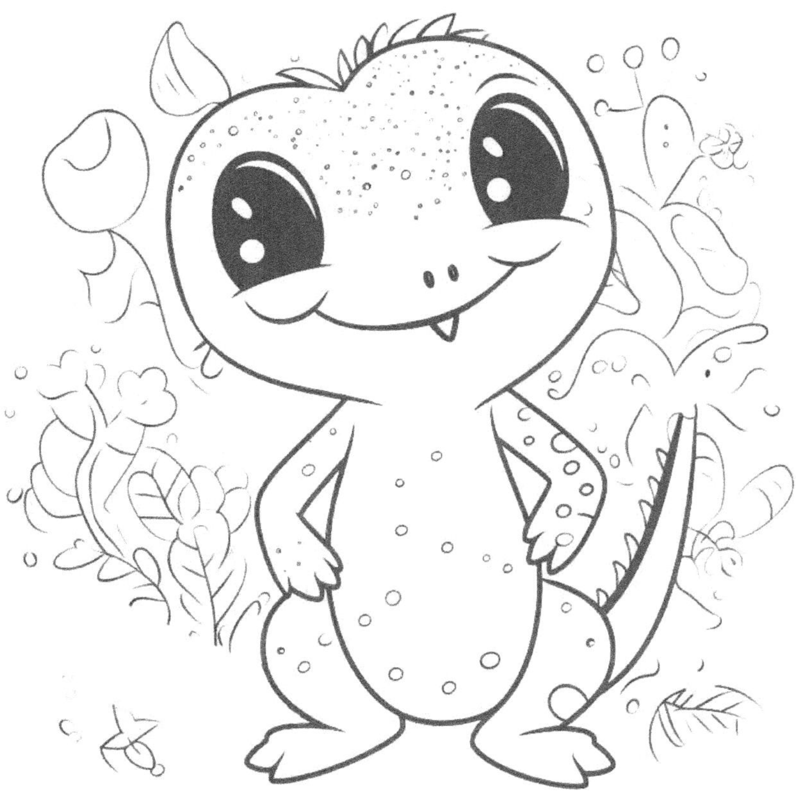

Frog

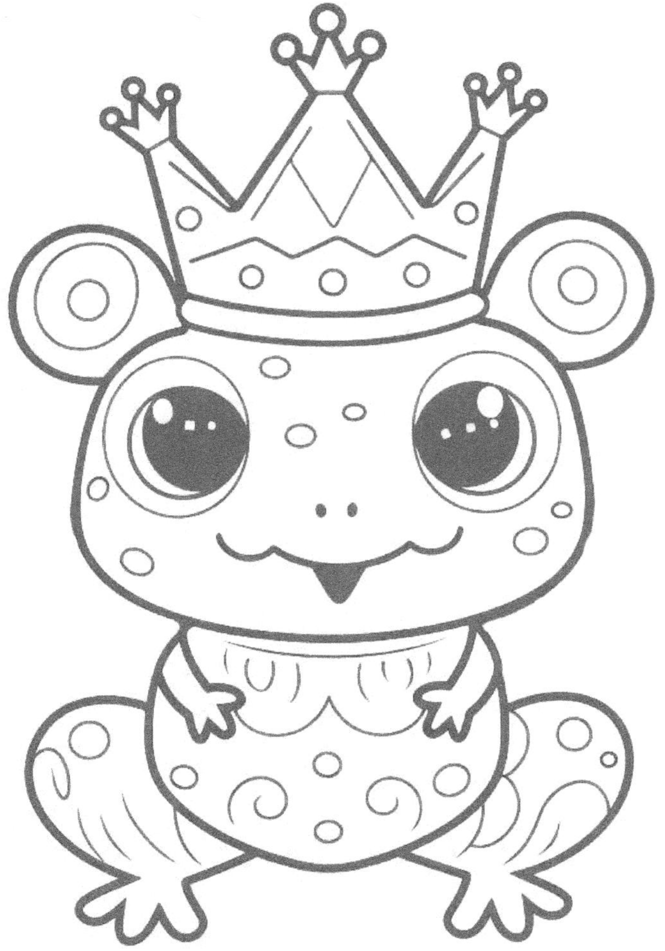

Flamingo

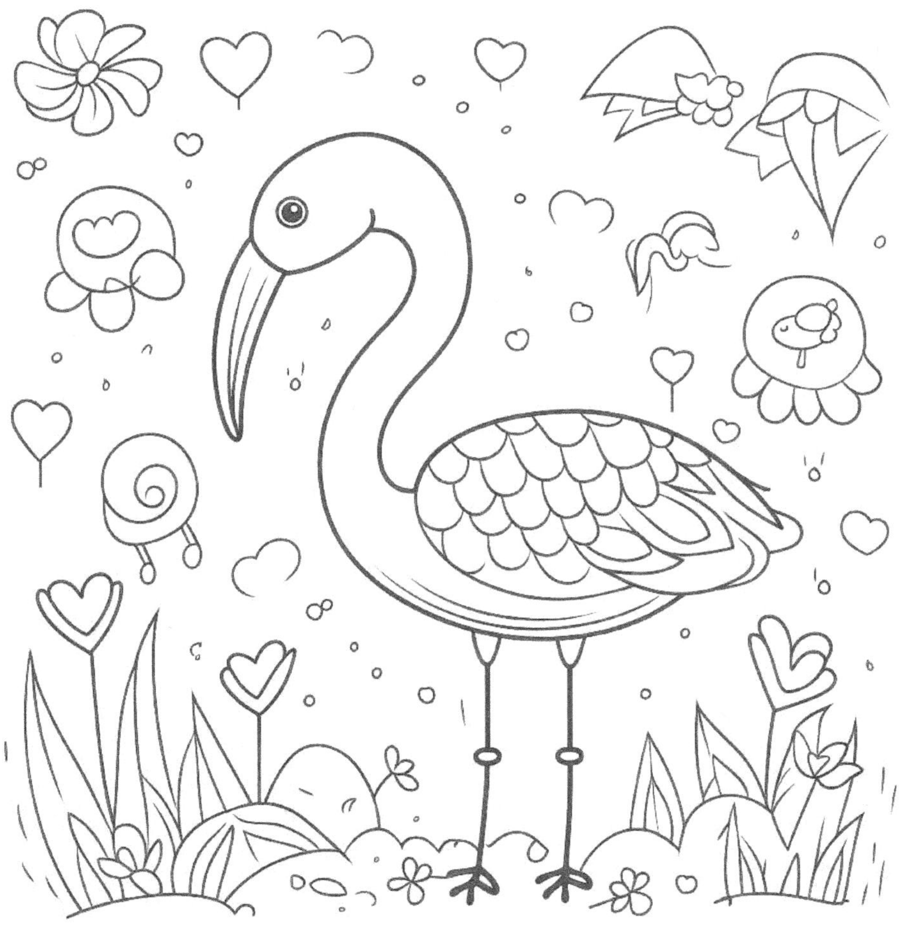

Peacock

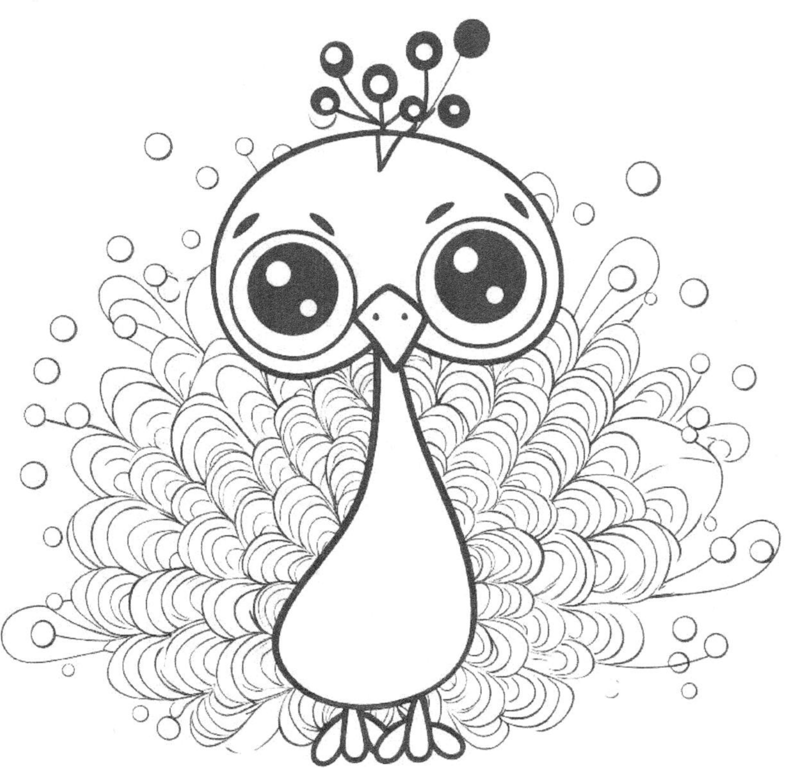

Raccoon

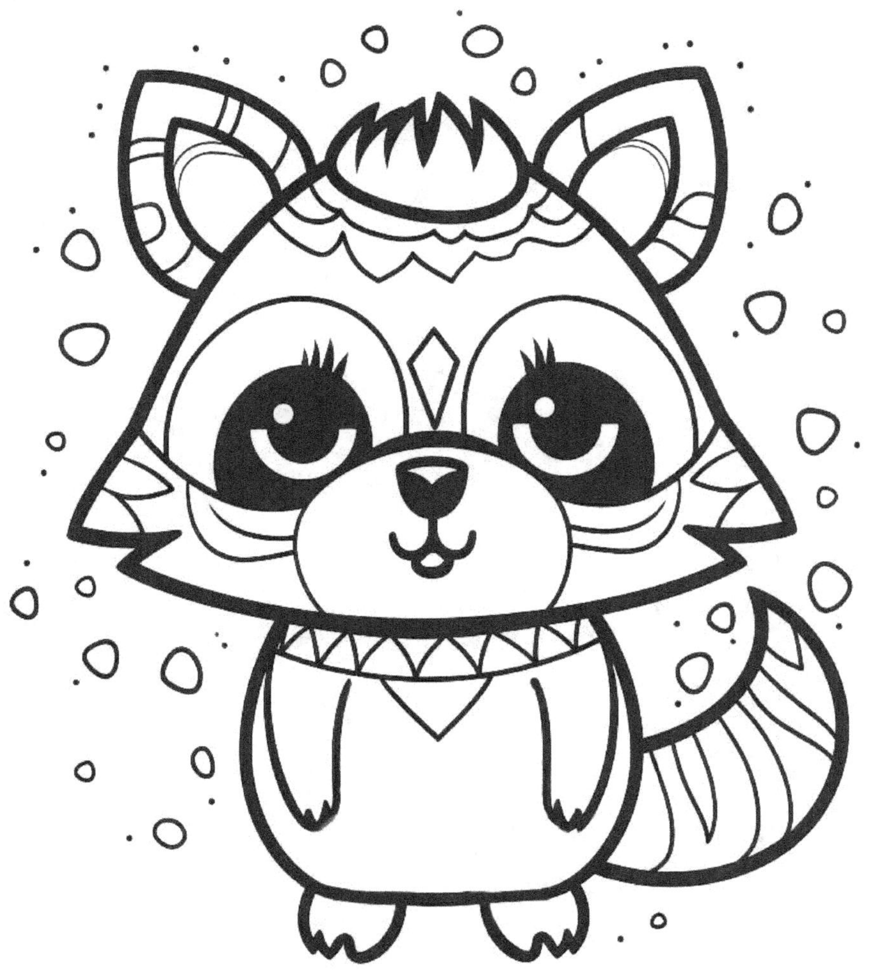

Squirrel

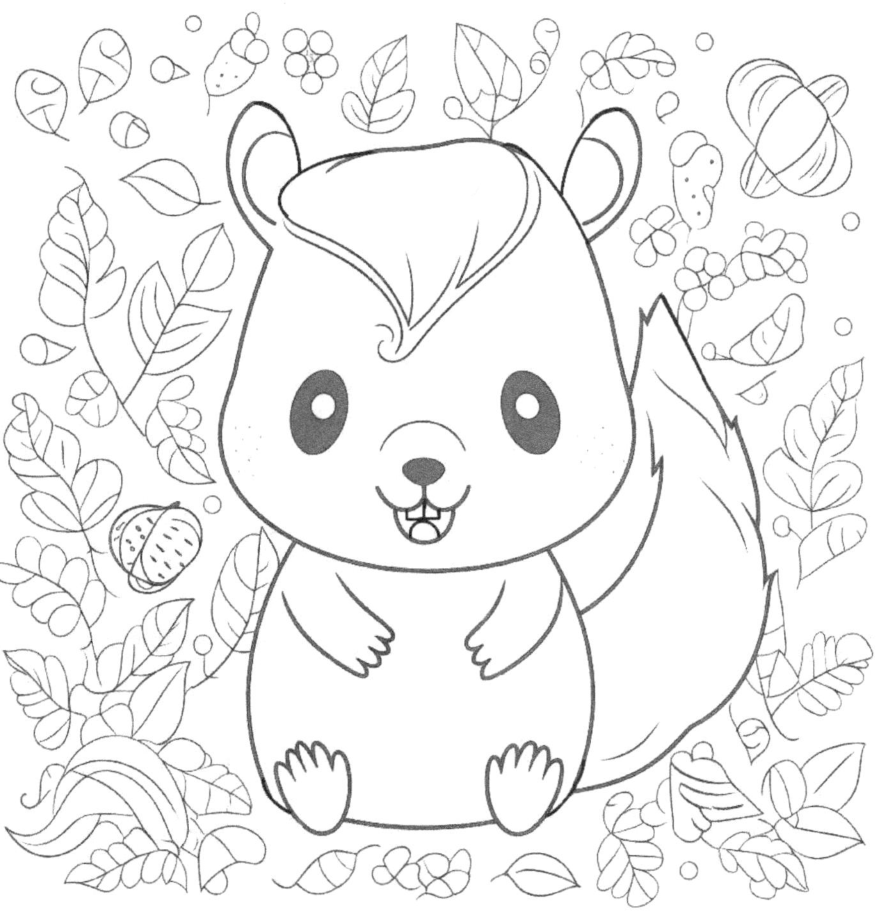

Toucan

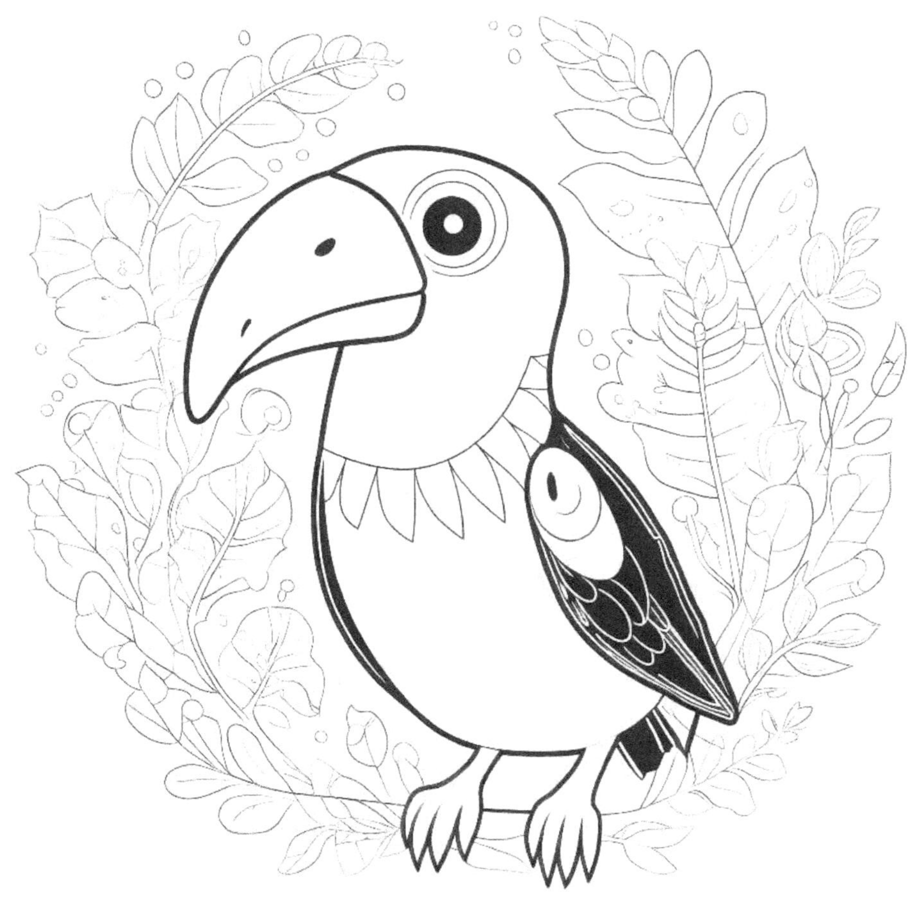

Fox

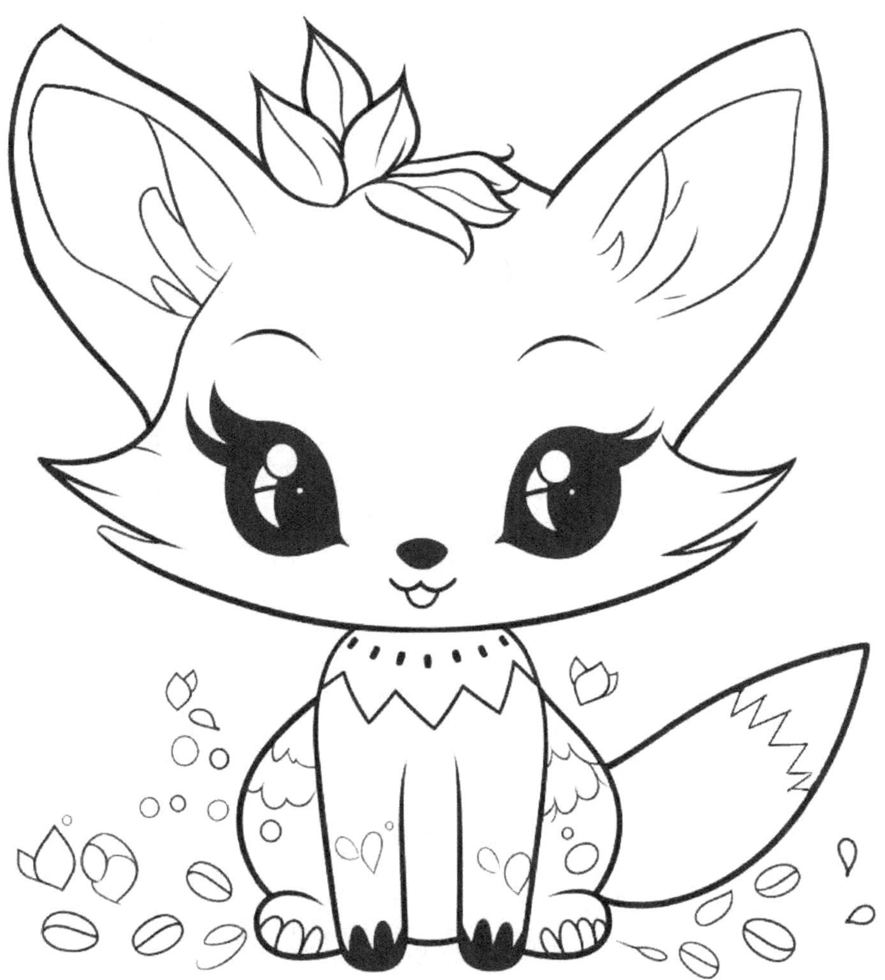